# Make a Living Living

Published in 2020 by
Laurence King Publishing Ltd
361–373 City Road
London EC1V 1LR
email: enquiries@laurenceking.com
www.laurenceking.com

Commissioned images by Daniel Balda, Julie Devarenne, Anna Rosa Krau,
Alex Maguire, Suzanne Pijnenburg, Shuhei Tonami and Dan Wilton are
credited in the Picture Credits on page 128.

This book was designed and produced by Laurence King Publishing Ltd,
London.

A catalogue record for this book is available from the British Library.
ISBN: 978 1 78627 582 0

Senior editor: Andrew Roff
Designer: Mariana Sameiro

Printed in China

Laurence King Publishing is committed to ethical and sustainable
production. We are proud participants in The Book Chain Project®
bookchainproject.com

# Make a Living
# LIVING

Nina Karnikowski

Laurence King Publishing

# CONTENTS

# INTRODUCTION

**If there's one thing social media has to answer for, it's making us think that extraordinary lives simply fall into people's laps.**

We're constantly bombarded with images of glossy, enviable-looking lives that seem both unattainable and inexplicable. We wonder how these people got to be doing what they do, and how they actually pay their bills.

I know this, because as a freelance travel writer who posts glossy, enviable-looking pictures on Instagram most days, the question I am asked most of all is: how on earth do you actually make money from travelling? And how can I do it, too?

Now, being a travel writer is an extraordinary way to make a living. I visit a dozen countries a year, on adventures mostly sponsored by travel companies who want their trips featured in the newspapers, magazines and websites I am then paid to write for. But I'd be lying if I told you making it happen was easy, because it wasn't.

For me it involved five years at university (using a AU $35,000/ US $24,700 student loan I'm still paying off) studying journalism and international studies, while doing unpaid work experience. After that came the begging – emailing contacts at the newspaper I wanted to work for, every week for months

on end. Finally they relented, and I toiled away there for five more years before a hallowed writer position opened up on the travel team, which allowed me to fulfil my dream of living in India for a year.

Eighteen months later, however, the newspaper underwent a restructure, and I was out of a job. At first I felt like my life was over, but I soon realized it was actually an enormous gift. Here was my chance to build the kind of life I'd only ever dared peek at from the corner of my eye, a life outside the nine to five.

First I spent AU $300 (US $200) creating a website using a developer based in Serbia, opened a travel-based Instagram account, and taught myself how to take better photos and videos to sell alongside my stories. Over that first year, while mostly using

my redundancy payout to cover rent, I built up freelance work and streamlined my life to keep overheads low. My husband and I moved into an old apartment on his family's farm a few hours from the city, which reduced outgoings, and did it up mostly with furniture donated by family and friends and flea-market finds. I stopped buying clothes, visiting the hairdresser and having expensive dinners, and held off buying the car I'd been saving for, so I could keep doing the work I loved.

Were the sacrifices worth it? Hell yes. Since then I've travelled to dozens of places – from Antarctica, India and Zambia to Japan, Nepal, Peru and beyond. These journeys have opened my mind and my heart and, in the act of writing about them, have hopefully helped my readers expand in a similar way.

from a chocolatier by the sea to a creative-network founder living on a boat. These people are telling the truth about the hard work and sacrifices that went into making their lives as remarkable as they are today, so you can make yours remarkable, too. Through their stories and tips, plus some dynamic exercises, you'll learn how to trust yourself, take risks, see the lessons in your failures and monetize your passions.

If you're looking to find fame or get rich quick, this isn't the book for you. But if you're wishing to take more pleasure in the simple things and minimize stress, to take control of your time and energy, to travel, cultivate inspiring relationships and build a successful, purpose-driven career doing what you love, then read on. This book is for you.

NK

There are downsides, of course. I've missed more weddings and birthdays than I can count, I'm not available nearly as much as I'd like to be for family and friends, I get tired and sick more than I would otherwise and I make less money than almost all my friends. But I really love the work I do. It feeds me intellectually, creatively and spiritually, and it affords me a lifestyle I couldn't even have imagined as a kid.

Here's the thing: you can make a living living, too. You may not believe that you have the tools you need to do it, but this book is here to give them to you. It will help you craft your own creatively fulfilling life, one you don't need a vacation to escape from, and prove to you that making a living and making

a life don't have to point in opposite directions.

To make that happen, I chatted with 26 creatives from around the world about how they achieved their ideal existence, from a potter in the bush to a woodcarver on an island, and

## Emica Penklis

The chocolatier
on having a purpose

# 'Follow your dreams – it's the only way you'll be truly fulfilled.'

For 35-year-old Emica Penklis, chasing her dream of creating a handcrafted, organic chocolate company that actually enhances the consumer's wellbeing hasn't been an easy road. But take a peek inside her life today, running her thriving business Loco Love in the Australian surf town of Byron Bay, and you'll realize that any struggles have been well worth it.

Since starting Loco Love using a AU $1,000 (US $700) tax rebate in 2013, Emica has funnelled both the knowledge of health and the human body she learned from studying naturopathy for three and a half years, and almost every cent earned working part-time jobs, into building her business. She has taught herself everything she knows – from how to actually make chocolate that's vegan, gluten- and refined sugar-free using superfoods and tonic herbs, to creating invoices and doing accounts, learning about marketing, designing a commercial kitchen, creating packaging, managing staff and more. Along the way there have been machinery breakdowns, suppliers going bankrupt, copycat companies and customers baulking at the idea of 'healthy' chocolate that comes with a higher price tag.

Societal doubt about following a non-traditional path is something else Emica has had to contend with. 'When I started Loco Love, my partner at the time often ridiculed the idea, especially when it came to it delivering financially. Friends and family were supportive, but everyone was shocked I could actually make a living making chocolate,' says Emica. 'Still today, as much as I don't like to admit this, being a young and relatively inexperienced woman in business means people often don't take you seriously until you prove you're professional, by being reliable and consistent in every aspect of the business.'

The huge highs have made up for all of this, though: building her own chocolate factory in Byron Bay, which she now runs with her husband, being featured in *Vogue* magazine and, the biggest one of all, making a living doing what she loves. She works with her hands as she'd fantasized about doing since she was a kid, can work to her own timeline, is surrounded by a community of inspiring business owners and is able to live by the ocean, in her favourite part of the world.

'I spent so many years not understanding or accepting the society we live in. We work in jobs we hate, for money to buy things we don't need, and everyone's walking around complaining all the time,' says Emica. 'Finally, it dawned on me that it's only by being the most authentic, inspired, love-filled version of yourself that you can help change the world, and that has become a big part of my company's ethos.'

If there's one thing we can learn from Emica, then, it's this. Following your heart and building your dream life – where you write your own rules and are free from societal strictures – won't mean your life will be free of struggle. But because you're doing something you love, and are living a life filled with purpose, that struggle will be completely worthwhile.

Emica's tips to
*make a living living:*

- <u>Get really honest with yourself</u> about what you want. Write it down.

- <u>Ask yourself: what can I contribute</u> that no one else can?

- Remember that <u>what you do</u>, more than what you say, <u>proves what you believe.</u>

LocoLove.com
@locolovechocolate

# Yuichi Takeuchi
The tiny-house builder
on simplifying life

*'Reduce the space you live in and you'll discover the life meant for you.'*

If there's one thing Yuichi Takeuchi wants people to learn from his work building tiny houses, it's to live with less so they can focus on what truly matters: family, community and nature.

Forty-five-year-old Yuichi started on his tiny-house path 12 years ago when, after living in London and Amsterdam for eight years making art and furniture while also working as a sushi chef, he returned to Japan. 'After being in those two big cities for so long, I arrived back in Japan and was immediately drawn to the forests,' he says.

He started designing environmental education programmes for kids in the mountainous Yamanashi prefecture. Wanting more people to come to the mountains, he built a treehouse for them to stay in, using skills he'd learned teaching kids to make shelters in the woods. It was a success and he continued building dozens of treehouses, eventually starting his business Tree Heads & Co. in 2010. Soon he shifted from treehouses to tiny homes. 'It was the tiny-house philosophy I loved most, that idea of encouraging people to simplify their lives,' he says.

Yuichi moved with his wife and two kids into a small house in the countryside three hours from Tokyo, and also built a tiny home on wheels that he uses as a mobile office and for family holidays. By living in this smaller space, says Yuichi, he and his family spend more time outside and have developed a stronger connection to nature, and to their community. 'People in the countryside have more relaxed lives, so they help each other. In the city I was too busy for that,' he says. 'Here I can design and build things for my neighbours in exchange for vegetables. We swap rather than relying on cash – life is much easier and more enjoyable.'

Yuichi's community came together to help him create a documentary he produced in 2017, called *Simplife*, on the US tiny-house movement. 'I'm just a builder – I couldn't shoot the movie, make the music or do the graphics and website, so local friends helped me create that film,' he says.

A passionate advocate for living at what he calls 'human scale', Yuichi believes in smaller spaces and fewer possessions. 'People are often surrounded by a lot of things that don't really make their life happy and they're working hard to buy those things,' he says. 'Living in a smaller space means you can only be surrounded by things you love, and you have fewer things to take care of, which means you have more time and energy for what really matters.'

Yuichi's tips to
*make a living living*:

- Look at the things you own and, like Marie Kondo suggests, <u>ask whether they make you happy</u>. Get rid of the ones that don't.

- <u>Find a community</u>. These people will help you and teach you new skills.

- <u>Make things you want</u> rather than buying them. It's much cheaper and unleashes creativity.

Treeheads.com
@treeheads_co

## Mukul Bhatia

The photographer and creative consultant
on being nomadic

# 'Plan the numbers, minimize spending, then dedicate all your energy to your idea.'

'To look at travel sites and see all the places I could go and imagine the projects I could do there, that brings me so much more joy than any material thing ever could,' says 30-year-old Indian Mukul Bhatia.

It's largely this non-materialistic attitude that has helped Mukul to get where he is today, travelling 80 per cent of the year to remote destinations, making a living from photographic projects and creative consulting for sustainable companies.

A fearless pursuit of the new and different has also been crucial to Mukul's trajectory. After finishing his master's degree in photography and visual communications in Delhi at the age of 21, he embarked on a seven-month journey across India, living with tribes in Rajasthan, hippies in Goa, transgender sex workers in Pune and mystics at the Maha Kumbh Mela, one of the world's biggest spiritual gatherings. These travels defined his life's path and his creative voice. For two years afterwards he worked as a photojournalist for a digital media company, mostly covering the conflict in Kashmir. 'Living with war meant constantly facing the idea of mortality, which taught me important lessons about living your life exactly the way you want,' he says.

Inspired by these adventures, Mukul started an online anthropological project called Nomadic Origins in 2015. Funded by a grant from the textile company MATTER Prints that was supplemented by savings, it saw him photographing and writing about nomads in 21 countries, and taught him about website coding, location scouting, social media strategy and more.

During this time Mukul's Instagram presence grew, exposing his work and eccentric personal style to international brands. These brands now employ him for photography and creative consultancy, on all-expenses-paid jobs around the world. Mukul charges anywhere from US $1,500 to US $10,000 for his marketing, branding and social media strategies, and now also generates income from brand-sponsored posts on his Instagram.

While many may fetishize Mukul's nomadic lifestyle, he says it's not for everyone. 'Instagram doesn't reveal the downsides, like lack of routine and missing important events, and if you're not comfortable with being alone, chances are you'd hate it,' he says. 'But I love being in another person's shoes whose reality is far from mine, and to translate that in my work gives me a lot of satisfaction.'

Mukul chooses not to have a permanent home, staying with his family or in short-term rentals when he's back in Delhi. 'I spend my money on things that really make me happy – mostly travel and good food. It's not a sacrifice, it's choosing my priorities and not living on "auto" mode dictated by society,' he says. Mukul's life is less about accumulating material possessions, and more about 'curating millions of fables for future grandchildren'.

## Mukul's tips to *make a living living:*

- <u>Identify your strengths and weaknesses.</u> Write them down.

- Try searching 'Everywhere' on the Skyscanner search engine, and see how far you can go.

- Read *Wabi-Sabi* by Leonard Koren. It explores the Japanese notion of imperfect beauty and helps you <u>be happier with less</u>.

mukulbhatia.com
@foundintranslations

Left: *Banjara Woman* excerpt from *Nomadic Origins*, 2015
Below: Work from Kashmir, 2016

## Anne Schwalbe

The photographer and
artist on slow living

# 'Keep things simple and you'll save money and have more time to enjoy life.'

When the German photographer Anne Schwalbe bought a neglected 150-year-old countryside cottage two hours outside Berlin five years ago, she was excited rather than daunted by the idea of spending weekends working on it.

'I really like to work with my hands,' says the 45-year-old, who splits her time between the house and an apartment in the centre of Berlin. 'I look forward to the monotonous work of repairing the windows, weeding my garden, chipping wood and firing the oven. I appreciate these simple things.'

The simple things in life are a big source of inspiration for Anne's nature-based, ethereal analogue photography, in which she experiments with light and everyday subjects. She has now published five photography books, and her work is regularly exhibited in galleries around the world, from Tokyo and New York to Amsterdam and beyond.

Anne's path to becoming a photographer was by no means linear. She spent her twenties searching for the right fit, studying German literature and cultural studies at university, then working at a publishing house, a flower shop and a radio station. It wasn't until she turned 30 that she enrolled in a four-year photography course at the Ostkreuzschule in Berlin, and she has been working full-time as a freelance photographer and artist ever since. 'It would be much better for my bank account if I just had a normal 40-hour job in an office, but I really appreciate all the freedom I have, all the exciting projects I'm doing, and the interesting people I meet and places I see,' she says.

Anne has purposely kept things in her life lo-fi, both to save money and to encourage herself to slow down. She doesn't have a dishwasher, for example, preferring to take her time doing the dishes by hand, and also doesn't have a car, which makes her get outside and run or ride her bike between places. This slow-living philosophy has also helped Anne create extra income streams to supplement her photography. Having taught herself to sew in order to make her own clothes, she now sells her handmade sweaters in her online store, along with her artworks and photography books. She also grows food and flowers in her wild, two-and-a-half-acre garden, which led her to become the garden columnist for the German magazine *Zeit* in early 2018.

'For a long time I wasn't happy and had a strong longing for something, but I didn't know what it was,' says Anne. 'My self-confidence wasn't great so I told myself I couldn't do things, like fashion design or photography. Now that everything has come together, I can hardly believe I thought that way.'

Anne's tips to
*make a living living*:

- <u>Stop saying yes to things you don't want to do.</u>

- Try to <u>do more things by hand</u>. It will keep you calm and save you money.

- When things get complicated, remember the German word *weitermachen*, which means keep going. <u>Begin the work, and keep going</u>.

Anneschwalbe.de
@anneschwalbe

*GARTEN (Silberblatt)*, 2018

# Mind map your life

It's time to get a bit Marie Kondo on your life. Time to get back to basics and get rid of all the mess. Mind mapping is a great tool for this, as it identifies the biggest drains on your three most precious resources – time, money and energy.

Take a blank page and write your name in the centre. From there, draw three branches: one each for time, money and energy. Next, draw lots of smaller branches off these three, each representing something that saps that particular resource. When you're done, study your map to see what your biggest time, money and energy vampires are, then start reclaiming them so you can use your time as efficiently as possible.

In response to the **time** branch of my mind map, for example, I set up rules for myself about logging off email and social media for specific periods each day. I also looked for help on the domestic side of things. Although that meant spending a little more money, it helped increase my productivity, which brought in more income. In response to **money**, I looked through the last six months of bank statements and cancelled a few non-essential direct debits, cut down on eating out and came up with some creative cost-free ways of spending my down time. As for **energy**, I made a conscious effort to think more positively and to surround myself with upbeat people.

Mind mapping is something you should do regularly, even monthly. This way, as you edge closer to achieving your goals, you can constantly review and streamline your progress.

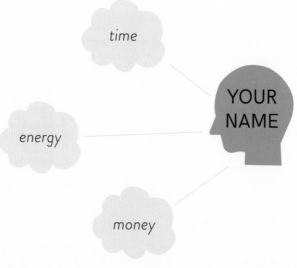

Here, you can see where my time and money are going, and what my energy drains are.

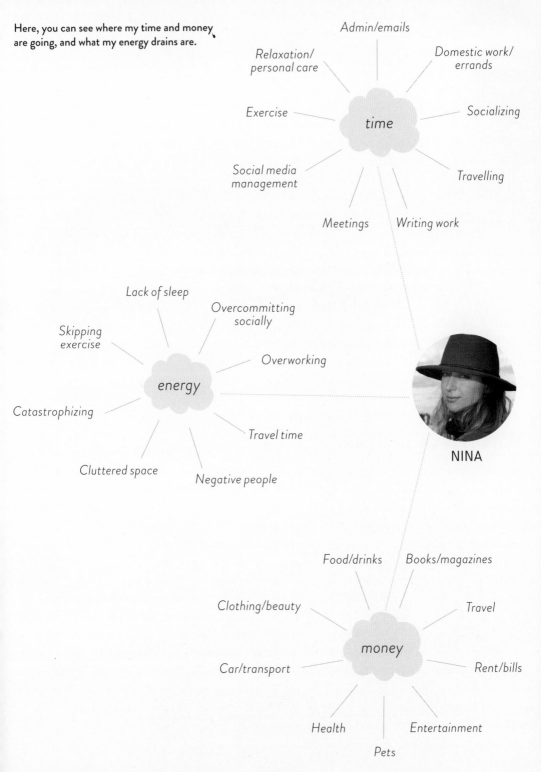

time
- Admin/emails
- Relaxation/personal care
- Domestic work/errands
- Exercise
- Socializing
- Social media management
- Travelling
- Meetings
- Writing work

energy
- Lack of sleep
- Overcommitting socially
- Skipping exercise
- Overworking
- Catastrophizing
- Travel time
- Cluttered space
- Negative people

NINA

money
- Food/drinks
- Books/magazines
- Clothing/beauty
- Travel
- Car/transport
- Rent/bills
- Health
- Entertainment
- Pets

## Pip Jamieson

The creative-network founder
on blending work and play

# 'Make your passion your job, and it will never feel like work again.'

Discovering a way to blend work and life was a major motivator behind Pip Jamieson founding her creative network The Dots, often referred to as a LinkedIn for the creative industry, in 2014. 'I was looking for that work–life blend, as opposed to work–life balance, because the latter implies you shouldn't like your work and that you work to live,' says the 40-year-old London-based creative.

Finding a solution to a problem she noticed while working as head of marketing at MTV was also part of what inspired Pip to start her company. 'Loads of my mates were adopting freelance careers or had side hustles and valued different things than getting paid loads, like working with nice people, wanting to enjoy life and having a purpose, but there was no easy way for them to find collaborators,' she says.

In 2009, Pip threw herself into solving this issue by starting a creative-network company called The Loop, which she exited in 2012, before starting The Dots. 'My business partner and I started brainstorming the idea at the pub after work and when we felt it had legs, we quit our MTV jobs and sank our life savings into bringing the platform to life. To be honest, we had no idea what we were doing,' she laughs, adding that for nine months before launching they 'relied on trial and error, worked all hours and lived on tinned tuna'.

'I've worn so many hats since starting The Dots,' says Pip, listing strategist, negotiator, marketer, product manager, salesperson and finance manager as some of them. 'So early on, I got into the habit of devouring roughly a book a week on subjects I didn't fully understand, listening to them on Audible while I walked to work.'

Running The Dots has allowed Pip finally to achieve the work–life blend. She gets to speak at the creative conferences she used to fork out hundreds of pounds to attend, is asked to galleries and exhibitions she once lusted after being invited to, and travels internationally year-round, all in the name of work.

Running a company with 25 employees can, of course, be stressful. There have been crashing servers, investment hiccups, bad hiring decisions and more. But Pip focuses on viewing these as opportunities to learn, remains resolutely positive and, believing that 'the people you surround yourself with are everything, on a personal and work level', she draws people around her who do the same.

Aside from daily meditation, a key element to Pip's maintaining a sense of calm is living and often working on her houseboat, which she and her husband bought in 2014 and which she says is also one of the most affordable ways to live in London. 'I walk onto the boat and stress just disappears,' she says.

## Pip's tips to *make a living living*:

- Read the book *Ikigai*, about the Japanese concept of <u>finding that thing you love, you're good at, you get paid for, and that the world needs</u>.

- <u>Immerse yourself in events</u>: it's a great way to <u>be inspired and build connections</u>. There are a heap on The Dots.

- <u>Build a portfolio of mentors,</u> experts on different topics you need covered, so you're not relying too heavily on one person.

the-dots.com
@the_dots_uk

# Nicole Leybourne

The knitter
on using the internet

## 'Look online and you'll discover how to create almost anything.'

In two and a half years, New Zealander Nicole Leybourne went from teaching herself to knit from YouTube videos, to receiving an order from Net-a-Porter for 600 of her hand-knitted mohair and woollen jumpers, which retail for up to US $585 a piece.

'I was completely self-taught, I didn't study textiles or anything like that,' says the 28-year-old, who splits her time between her home town of Auckland in New Zealand and Lima in Peru, where most of her production is based. 'Still now, if I have an idea of a different stitch or something I want to do, I'll teach myself on YouTube,' she says.

Feeling dissatisfied while studying natural medicine at university in 2015, Nicole decided to throw herself into her knitting hobby. She started making knits for friends, set up an Instagram account and created a website. Six months later she was receiving more orders than she could fulfil, so she put her studies aside to knit full-time. She moved in with her parents to minimize overheads, and invested her savings in employing other local knitters, 'a lot of middle-aged and elderly women who loved knitting'. When her business grew to a point where she was struggling to keep up with demand, Nicole decided to move production to Peru, from where she had been sourcing her yarns.

Nicole and her partner, who works for The Knitter, now rent an apartment in Lima for three months a year so they can oversee production of the knits, which are hand-woven in Peruvian homes. 'We put all our things in storage when we aren't staying in one city, and only sign short-term leases,' she says. 'That allows us flexibility, and it's nice not having to worry about owning a heap of stuff and being able to leave when we need a change of scenery.'

There have still been hard times, says Nicole. Times when she has been 'living off potatoes and eggs', when she has felt overwhelmed by the never-ending to-do list that comes with being her own boss, and the huge learning curves involved in fulfilling bulk orders like Net-a-Porter's. But, she says, it's completely worthwhile. 'You do make sacrifices – I don't own a car or property or any of those things you're supposed to own – but it feels amazing to be able to give my Peruvian knitters work so they can support their families, and I'm always happy. I still regularly pinch myself that I get to do this as a job.'

Nicole's tips to
*make a living living:*

- The internet really helps with growing a business. <u>You don't need a lot of money</u> to start, just an idea.

- Just <u>get in there</u> and do the thing you want to do, because you'll never *feel* ready.

- If you're in a job you don't love, <u>spend just half an hour a day</u> on what you'd prefer to be doing until you're ready to leap. And <u>save as much money</u> as you can.

theknitter.co
@theknitter

## Graeme Corbett

The florist on faking
it till you make it

'Fake it for
a while if you're
unsure – you likely
know more than
you think.'

When clients arrive at Graeme Corbett's floristry studio and discover it's actually the garage below his London apartment, they're usually shocked. 'Even though I'm very transparent about the fact that it's just me, people often still think I'm a really big business,' laughs the 35-year-old.

While working in the TV industry, where he spent 12 years as a casting director on shows including *Big Brother* and *The Voice*, Graeme realized the importance of pursuing his dreams. 'I used to listen to people sing, and regardless of how brilliant or terrible they were, they all knew exactly what they wanted and weren't going to give up,' he says. 'I'd sit there and think, well this is fun, but I don't have the passion they do.'

Graeme started experimenting with business ideas during time off work. He created an Etsy shop selling revamped flea-market finds, then started a pickle company, before finally quitting his TV job and enrolling in a two-week floristry course. 'I did the cheapest I could find, thinking I could learn the basics and decide if I liked it,' he says.

He loved the course, and found a nine-month paid internship afterwards through a florist he admired on Instagram. 'The very traditional flower school I'd done the course with was appalled, saying, "This woman isn't a real florist, she's just faking it." But my thinking was, it doesn't matter if she's classically trained, she's creating gorgeous work and people are paying for it.'

The internship taught him everything, from making bouquets and wedding arrangements to writing proposals and pricing structures. Once he finished, he launched his own floristry business, Bloom + Burn, using his spare bedroom as his studio and building his own website using Wix.

'In that first year, I'd invest in buying from the markets once a week even if I didn't have a job on, just to build relationships with the traders,' he says. 'I'd come home and play with the flowers, then put my creations on Instagram. I was almost faking it a bit, to get people to notice what I was doing and to improve my skills.'

It worked. By 'saying yes to everything' in his first year, Graeme built his client base, and in his second year he booked 50 weddings. 'I wasn't making much money on most jobs that first year, but they were all worth taking, because that's how I trained myself and developed my style,' he says.

Graeme has now got enough of a reputation that he can charge more for his work, and do less of it. 'You watch shows like *The Apprentice* that say, "If you're not working 24 hours a day it's never going to happen." But I'm not looking to build a multi-million-pound business,' he says. 'My goal is to make enough money so I'm comfortable, I'm doing interesting work, and I'm having a good time doing it.'

Graeme's tips to
*make a living living*:

- When you're starting out, you may need to <u>take work that doesn't pay much</u> so you can <u>learn by experience</u>. The better you get, the more you can charge.

- <u>Look for clever ways to use your space</u>, instead of paying for expensive storefronts, workshops or offices.

- Just <u>try the thing you've been dreaming of</u> doing, because finding the right fit might take a few attempts.

bloomandburnflowers.com
@bloomandburn

# Be your own tutor

In our internet-fuelled world, expensive degrees or diplomas are less essential to becoming masters of our craft than ever before. By following these four steps, you'll be able to teach yourself almost everything you need to know.

## 1

### CREATE YOUR 'COLLEGE'

*By this, I mean a dedicated space for learning. A small desk in the corner of your bedroom, an unused garage – just a designated space to get you straight into the learning mindset.*

## 2

### SET GOALS

*First, write down your end goal – 'become a florist', for example. Below that, list all the major topics you'll need to learn to get you there: the basics of floral design, time management, processing orders, marketing, etc. Next, commit to a set period of time each day (whatever you can manage, even if that's only half an hour each night) to start ticking these off.*

# 3

## RESEARCH

*Every day when you sit down at your 'college', research one thing on your list. It's as simple as plugging 'floral design basics' into Google – whatever topic you're attacking, you can rest assured there are books and articles, YouTube tutorials, audiobooks and podcasts, or online courses on sites such as CreativeLive or Udemy. Jot down questions as you go, then answer them, too.*

# 4

## GET FEEDBACK

*Whether it's a tutor, coach or mentor, you'll eventually need to enlist the help of someone who's been there, done that, to make sure you're on track. Emailing people you look up to for small bits of advice, rather than lumping it all on one person, is a great approach.*

# 'Don't copy anyone else; people can feel it when you're not sincere.'

We've all dreamt about it: pulling up sticks and renovating a home somewhere wildly exotic. Having the guts and vision to do it, however, is another story. Two who did are the Parisians Cyrielle and Julien, who worked in fashion – Cyrielle as a photographer and model, Julien as an art director – for over a decade before escaping to Morocco.

Having travelled to Marrakesh regularly since 2010, a city they loved for its energy and vibrancy, the couple's crunch point came in 2016. 'We were flying back to grey and rainy Paris one day when we made the decision to stay in Marrakesh and start a business. Within a month we were back in Morocco looking at properties,' says Julien.

After months of searching the couple found Riad Jardin Secret tucked down a quiet alleyway in the chaotic medina, and threw their life savings into purchasing it and transforming it into a soulful guesthouse and artists' residency. It would function, they decided, as both a thriving business and a place to feed their passions – for Cyrielle, her analogue photography and floral arranging; for Julien, his illustrations and working on his motorbike. It was a tremendous gamble, one they didn't tell their family and friends about until just a few weeks before they left Paris. 'We knew they would try to talk us out of it, and they did,' says Julien. 'They were like, "Maybe you're going to lose all of your previous work, your network, your clients."'

Cyrielle and Julien managed to quell the concerned voices, but that's when the hard work began. They spent the next eight months tirelessly restoring the six-bedroom home and giving it their own bohemian twist, working all hours seven days a week to find and manage the right workers and staff,

source all the decorations and plants, build the website, photograph the riad and more.

Their dedication paid off. Riad Jardin Secret quickly became a thriving hideaway and artists' residence that attracts creative guests from around the world, who pay up to EUR 260 (US $290) a night to stay there. For the first three years it was also home for the couple, who eventually moved to the countryside with their now two-year-old son.

Cyrielle and Julien continue happily working seven days a week to ensure the team at Riad Jardin

Secret is the best it can be, and that the riad continues to attract loyal guests and high occupancy rates, which Julien says they achieve by staying true to their vision. 'Because we still take care of every single detail, from the website and Instagram page, to the interior design and replying to guest emails, it's a real reflection of both of us. People definitely respond to that sincerity,' he says.

In addition to income from the riad, the couple have also been running their interior styling studio Rigotang since mid-2016, through which they redecorate and renovate Moroccan properties for clients.

Cyrielle and Julien's tips to
*make a living living:*

- <u>Be real and stay true to
yourself.</u>

- <u>Visiting museums and
meeting other creatives</u>
are both great sources of
inspiration.

- <u>Touch the edges of your
comfort zone</u> on a regular
basis. It will help you realize
what you're capable of.

riadjardinsecret.com
rigotang.com
@riadjardinsecret

## Asteria Malinzi

The fine art photographer
on learning to fail

# 'Don't let "no" stop you. You will be rejected for a reason – listen and learn.'

Rejection and failure are a crucial part of any creative career. This is something the 29-year-old Tanzanian Asteria Malinzi, whose photography is sold internationally and who runs the Artists Residency of Kigamboni (ARK) in Tanzania, learned early on. 'Growing up, my father's favourite word was no,' she says. 'He taught me that it's ok to be told no, and that you need to keep trying.'

Asteria became passionate about film photography while studying business management and marketing at university in England. 'I started teaching myself on a second-hand camera using YouTube, blogs and second-hand photography books, and I'd hang out at camera shops and ask people how they created their work,' she says. Meanwhile, she practised self-portraiture using a tripod in her student bedroom.

Once she finished her degree, Asteria enrolled in a two-year course at the Cape Town School of Photography. 'I learned all the things you need to actually sell your work, including website hosting, approaching galleries and buyers, writing grant proposals, marketing, pricing and more,' she says.

Asteria then started, quite literally, chasing internships. When the owner of the prestigious Erdmann Contemporary gallery spoke at her college, Asteria chased her into the elevator to convince her she needed her help. This woman not only gave Asteria her first internship and became her mentor, but also exhibited her work in the gallery.

When an artist's residency in Brazil that Asteria had been accepted into was cancelled at the last minute, she used the disappointment as fuel to design a residency in Tanzania. Not having the necessary finances, she pitched the idea to a

contact she met while working at a Kenyan gallery who was venturing into the hospitality industry, convincing them they should hire her to run an artist's residency on their 130-acre seaside estate. 'The idea started from a very selfish place,' she admits. 'I was bitter about that Brazilian residency and thought, "If you're not going to give it to me, I'll give it to myself."'

Creating the residency has meant Asteria has had to learn a whole new skill set, from working with building contractors and interior designers to sourcing

materials and organizing budgets. But her hard work has paid off. She now lives in the stunning seaside property free of charge, with the time and space she needs to produce more work, all while receiving a pay packet and empowering other local artists to do the same.

Meanwhile, enlisting the help of a manager has ensured her artworks continue to sell. 'Having someone who works hard to sell my work while I'm busy, who pushes me to keep creating and who I'm accountable to, has been invaluable,' she says.

Asteria's tips to
*make a living living*:

- <u>Learn to be ok with 'no'.</u>
  Remember that doors
  close so others can open.

- <u>Get a manager.</u> All
  creatives need someone to
  stay accountable to.

- <u>Intern as much as possible</u>,
  to expand your contacts
  and skill set.

asteriamalinzi.com
@justcallmesimba

*Take My Soul*, 2015

## Rhiannon Griego

The weaver
on experimentation

# 'Experiment in whatever way you can – we are all creative.'

Experimentation is the key to unlocking creativity, says weaver Rhiannon Griego. And she should know. Because to reach where she is today, weaving clothing and art pieces and making jewellery under her label Rhiannon Griego (formerly Ghost Dancer) in her home in the Californian mountains, she had to follow her own path of discovery.

Feeling a little lost while studying interior design at college, Rhiannon took off travelling across the US, experimenting with jewellery-making along the way. When she found a mentor who inspired her to 'make the final jump as a maker', she began making a living from her jewellery, selling on Etsy and at artisanal markets and trade shows.

After five years of jewellery-making, however, the now 37-year-old hit a wall. 'I started experimenting again with other creative pathways, and within a week I found my weaving teacher, took a class and was hooked,' she says. 'Being taught directly by people like this is my strongest recommendation when it comes to learning the ropes.'

Having already learned how to price her jewellery from basic online formulas, and having established an audience through online networking, Instagram and local shows, Rhiannon followed the same process with her weaving. Since she creates by hand, she scouted for higher-end stores to support the price point of her weavings, which can retail for as much as US $6,600, and started wholesaling to brands including Free People. 'Wholesaling my work is what drew a strong audience,' she says. 'I've always chosen stores with a fitting price point, that respect me by paying promptly and educate the client on my work. This is all imperative when it comes to creative business relationships,' she says.

Rhiannon often works up to 14 hours a day weaving her intricate creations by hand, and also runs regular workshops to educate aspiring weavers and to boost her income. But because she's her own boss she can craft her days as she pleases, leaving time for exercise and hanging out with friends and family.

Finding flow in her work, which she describes as a moving

meditation, has also been key to Rhiannon's success. 'Weaving is very methodical, and when you're really engaged in the process you can reach that place of Zen.' Quieting her thoughts through the process of weaving also helps to 'provide a sense of calm when my mind finds concern with the less than conventional life I've chosen,' she says.

Rhiannon's tips to
*make a living living*:

- <u>Find local business and
  art classes</u>, and <u>keep
  experimenting creatively</u>
  until you find the right fit.

- <u>Follow brands whose
  style resonates</u> with you,
  and write down what you
  appreciate about them.

- Once you've found the
  brands and artists you love,
  email to <u>ask if they're open
  to an apprenticeship</u>, or
  take them for coffee to
  pick their brains.

rhiannongriego.com
@rhiannonmgriego

# From mimic to master

As Picasso said, 'good artists copy, great artists steal', and it's true that all creative work builds on what came before it. If you're finding it difficult to begin the process of creating, you can start by dissecting the work of those you admire, then trying to emulate it.

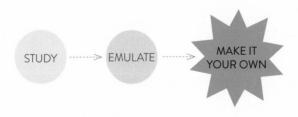

**Say you want to be a writer. Follow these steps in order to start your own work.**

## STUDY

Assemble a list of the writers you respect most, and buy or borrow their best books.

## MAKE IT YOUR OWN

Next, create your own imitations of your favourite works, emulating their styles but incorporating your own ideas and flair to make work that's completely yours.

## EMULATE

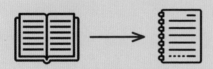

Copy passages from these authors to examine how they create – their pacing, voice, word choice, etc. Summarize what you learn as you go, jotting your notes down in a book you can look at as a refresher later.

This method works with products, too. Imagine you want to create your own line of herbal teas: collect your favourite packets, study the ingredients, try recreating them until you understand the method, then experiment with creating your own, specific to your tastes and style. Think of it like learning a musical instrument – you start out by playing other people's songs while you master your technique, right?

Whatever creative pursuit you choose, whether it's pottery, floristry, woodworking, painting or making music, it's the same process: study, emulate, make it your own.

# Julia Khan Anselmo

The dinner party host
on embracing the unknown

# 'Step outside your comfort zone and see how you feel and react.'

The first step off the conventional path and towards your ideal lifestyle sometimes isn't so much a step as a push. When Julia Khan Anselmo was made redundant from her job at an art consultancy in her native Canada seven years ago, she was forced to begin digging deep to discover what she really wanted to do with her life.

'I examined what I was doing in my down time that brought me joy, rather than focusing on what job I thought I should get because of my art history degree, or to please my parents, make money, or fit into society,' says the 35-year-old.

Realizing that cooking, hosting and connecting inspiring women was what she spent most of her free time doing, Julia held her first Feisty Feast – a five-course dinner for 12 women – in her Vancouver apartment one month later. 'I was fully in flow and time just slipped away that night, and afterwards I felt really elated and excited. I'd never felt that in any

of the jobs I'd done before,' she says. 'That's when I knew I'd hit something special that I needed to pursue.'

Julia now runs quarterly Feisty Feasts for up to 120 women in unique settings around the world – from a Moroccan furniture store in San Francisco, or a ceramics atelier in Vancouver, to an old dairy in London – incorporating guest speakers including filmmakers, designers and writers, and workshops run by local makers. After deducting all the expenses involved in throwing these events, however, Julia realized Feisty Feast wasn't

yet making enough money for her to live on. So in 2017 she launched a second brand, a horse-hair accessories label called Laasso, and also started doing freelance styling work for extra income.

Patience and positivity, says Julia, have been key to getting her where she is now. 'There are times when I have to fight against things like negative self-talk, and remember that it's ok for things to take time,' she says. 'I've spoken with other creatives who've said it took them ten years to make good money doing what they love, so you just have to keep doing it.'

Because she's her own boss, Julia was able to move to Amsterdam, a city she loves for its village atmosphere and vibrant community of artists and musicians, with her fiancé three years ago. 'I didn't overthink the move before we did it,' says Julia. 'But I think a creative life requires that, being able to let yourself go into the unknown, take risks and be ok with feeling uncomfortable.'

Julia's tips to
*make a living living*:

- <u>Observe what gets you into that 'flow state'</u>, when you lose time and don't think about other things.

- If you're really clear about your dreams and goals, you will achieve them. So <u>be careful what you focus on</u>.

- It takes time to make money out of doing something you love. <u>Don't be ashamed of getting an unsexy side job to make extra money</u>.

feistyfeast.ca
laasso.co
@feisty_feast

# Aleph Geddis

The woodcarver
on making life a creative act

# 'Keep your eyes fresh and your brain engaged by living creatively in different spaces.'

For the woodcarver Aleph Geddis, living a creative life means not simply making art, but making every aspect of each day creative. The 46-year-old splits his year between Orcas Island in Washington state, Bali in Indonesia, Bulgaria's Rhodope mountains and Hokkaido in northern Japan, surrounding himself with inspiring creatives in each place and carving wherever he goes.

Born and raised on Orcas Island, Aleph began his woodcarving apprenticeship with his stepfather, also a carver, when he was 20. 'I'd spend half the year apprenticing and half the year travelling very cheaply, so travel became a big part of my creative process, keeping me inspired and my work fresh,' he says.

At the age of 30, Aleph opened a successful vintage store filled with wares from his travels, but realized the business was leaving him with less and less time to carve. 'Eventually I made a very conscious leap to close the store, take a big pay cut, move back to living very simply and focus fully on my art,' he says.

It was difficult at first, especially financially. But with time and with help from online platforms like Instagram, his carving took off. Aleph now exhibits and sells his artworks globally, including to clients like Facebook and the American outdoor clothing brand Filson. He also mentors and teaches carving, and most importantly enjoys creating his works. 'There's so much screen time and living in the abstract these days, so to do something very tangible, taking a rough piece of wood and turning it into a piece of art just through your focus and presence, that's really important.'

Rotating environments throughout the year is an essential part of Aleph's creative process. He built a small studio and living space on his friend's property in Bali, purchased his Bulgarian farmhouse, which he renovated with the help of friends, for a reasonable EUR 30,000 (US $33,700), and lives on his family's property on Orcas Island when he's home. 'There are a lot of really affordable places you can move to outside major cities; it's a lot easier to live nomadically than people might think,' he says.

Enjoying each hour of every day rather than just small parts of it is, according to Aleph, essential to making a living living. 'I think it's very important to focus on experience and how you're living your life, more than just the art, which is why I like to switch my surroundings,' he says. 'Otherwise creating art just becomes business. Of course we all need to make money, but then you're almost living a nine-to-five life, even though you're doing something creative.'

Aleph's tips to
*make a living living:*

- <u>Travel.</u> It's essential
  for maintaining a fresh
  perspective.

- <u>Apprentice</u> with somebody
  who's doing what you want
  to be doing.

- You can make your work
  and home environments
  really attractive without
  very much money, so
  brainstorm creative ways to
  <u>improve the space you're in,</u>
  like decorating with vintage
  furniture or plants.

alephgeddis.com
@alephgeddis

# Mattia Passarini

The tribal photographer
on balancing passion and diligence

# 'If you have a passion and the discipline to work at it every day, nothing is impossible.'

Scanning Mattia Passarini's Instagram account, filled with evocative photographs of remote tribes, the first question that springs to mind is how the 37-year-old Italian has the time and money to travel constantly to these far-flung corners of the globe.

Mattia started developing his photographic skills while working a nine-to-five sales job in Beijing, where he has been based since 2006. When an iconic Steve McCurry tribal photograph captured his attention on the wall of a local bar, he fell in love with the style and decided he wanted to create something similar. He connected with a group of local amateur photographers and began shooting with them at weekends, learning the basics as he experimented with style. It wasn't until he travelled to southern China, however, and discovered women still practising the ancient custom of foot binding, that he became fascinated by capturing disappearing cultures.

'In ten years, we may no longer see these people,' says Mattia of the dozens of tribes he has since visited in South Sudan, West Papua, Namibia and beyond. 'I'm compelled to document them in order to immortalize them in some way, and because they teach me important lessons, usually about how privileged our lives are in the modern world.'

When Mattia started his Instagram account in mid-2014, he began being contacted by other intrepid travellers who were interested in the trips he was taking to isolated parts of China, India, Myanmar and beyond. 'People started wanting to join me, they were curious about the remote places I was visiting,' says Mattia. 'I started to think, maybe I can do this as a business, taking people with me on my trips, and make money out of it while pursuing my photography.'

And that's exactly what he did. Initially, Mattia ran small group tours during his vacation time off work. When interest grew, he quit his job to start his travel company Remote Expeditions, using freelance site Fiverr to create a website for under US $2,000, and his Instagram following to attract clients. 'I didn't have a degree in travel management or anything, but it wasn't a crazy leap,' he says. 'I looked into the numbers and was completely sure about what I was doing when I started Remotexpeditions; I think that's very important.'

With itineraries designed by Mattia and led by local guides, Remotexpeditions now runs about 20 tours a year, providing the majority of his income and continuing to feed his wanderlust. This is supplemented by the sale of his photographic prints, which have received awards from the likes of *National Geographic*, and have been exhibited at the UNESCO headquarters, and sales of the Solarpop solar-powered lantern that he designed and launched in mid-2019.

## Mattia's tips to *make a living living:*

- <u>Set two or three goals each year,</u> so you know what you're working towards.

- <u>Instagram is essential – post every day.</u> Be patient while your audience grows, and <u>write engaging captions.</u>

- <u>Use freelancing sites</u> like Fiverr to get logos and websites done cheaply, <u>and funding platforms</u> like Kickstarter and Indigogo to finance creative projects.

mattiapassarini.com
remotexpeditions.com
@mattia_passarini

Above: *Smiling Monk*, Tibet, 2016
Left: *Yalimo*, West Papua, 2015

# Write your elevator pitch

To sell your work, you need to know your work. It sounds simple, but summarizing what makes your work unique and why people would want to invest in it, energetically or financially, isn't an easy task.

A helpful way of doing this is to write an 'elevator pitch', a 30-second spiel selling yourself and your work. In 100 words or less, answer the questions on the stopwatch opposite in as exciting and succinct a way as possible.

Focus on the 'why' behind what you do, making your responses personal. When you were a kid, did you spend hours in the art room at school, missing other classes and losing track of time, which is how you decided to become a painter? These sorts of personal life stories really hold people's attention and will get you to the core of your 'why'.

Perfect your elevator pitch before you do the other crucial set-up points, such as creating a website or Instagram account – because you can't do any of this well if you don't know exactly who you are and what drives you, first.

WHO ARE YOU?

WHAT DO YOU DO, AND HOW IS IT UNIQUE?

WHY WOULD I BUY OR SUPPORT YOUR WORK?

## Yenifer Canelón

The surf retreat founder
on trusting your instincts

# 'Self-belief helps you overcome perceived barriers, including distance and finance.'

As soon as you meet Yenifer Canelón, it becomes abundantly clear that the pint-sized Venezuelan has an extraordinary zest for life. It's no surprise, then, that her surf and yoga retreat Salti Hearts is aimed at helping women ignite that very spark in their own lives.

Growing up in the Venezuelan archipelago of Los Roques, Yenifer surfed her first wave when she was six years old. 'Once I'd done it, I got out of the water and told my mom, "I want to do this and nothing else for ever and ever"', she says.

And that's exactly what she has done. Yenifer studied oceanography on Venezuela's Isla Margarita, creating an NGO called Econatura 7 while she was there, then working for eight years in the Caribbean and Central America, mostly in marine conservation. By 27, Yenifer was ready for new challenges. She sold her boat, her car and most of her possessions and bought a one-way ticket to Bali. 'It wasn't easy leaving everything and everyone behind, but I knew I had to pursue my dream,' says the 35-year-old.

After arriving in Indonesia, Yenifer worked for three years as a surf photographer and instructor, saving money until she was ready to start her own women's surf retreat. 'Five months before my 30th birthday Salti Hearts was open, and I did 12 retreats in less than six months.'

Chasing a dream always comes with challenges, and Yenifer's came with plenty: starting from scratch, all alone, on the other side of the world; learning to speak Indonesian and understand Balinese culture; and setting up her business, with all the bureaucratic and financial strains that come with that, to name just a few.

'When I started Salti Hearts, I did everything,' she says. 'I was the host, the surf coach, the yoga teacher, the fitness adviser, the content creator, the social media manager, the administrator, the accountant. Not only because I had to be, to save costs, but also because I wanted to understand every area of my business, to make sure it grew organically and from the heart.'

After five years, Yenifer's business is now thriving, with her and her small team of six running two retreats a month in Indonesia and now also Mexico. Because her work is seasonal, Yenifer is able to take three months off each year during Bali's rainy season to strategize her business, and to travel to new surf destinations in the name of research.

Yenifer's tips to
*make a living living*:

- <u>Start each week with a 20-minute meeting with yourself.</u> Reflect on what's working and what isn't, and journal about what you want to achieve next week.

- <u>Podcasts are a great source of inspiration and motivation.</u> I love 'Water People' by Lauren L. Hill and Dave Rastovich.

- <u>See everyone who comes into your life as a teacher;</u> stay open to what you can learn from them.

saltihearts.com
@saltihearts

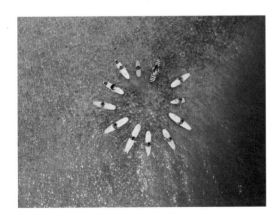

## Sarko Meené

The visual artist
on prioritizing freedom

# 'An artistic life means a free life, since you're no longer tethered to the 9 to 5.'

For the visual artist Sarko Meené, there is no such thing as a typical day. The 35-year-old's workload can vary widely depending on the artistic projects she's working on – from painting and sculpture exhibitions for the likes of Armenia's prestigious Cafesjian Center for the Arts, to large-scale installations for hotels, homes and restaurants. 'That's what a creative life is,' she says: 'not a steady boring run, but sprints and resting times.'

The sporting analogy is no accident. Before Sarko transitioned into the art world in 2013 she played tennis professionally for 16 years, eight of which she spent competing in the US, while simultaneously freelancing in event management. Her tennis background has helped her both financially, since she now coaches nutrition and personal training on the side, and also with her workflow as an artist. 'I only work on paintings when I have an exhibition coming up,' she says. 'My tennis background has taught me how to accelerate in bursts like that, because if I work every day on my art I'm going to exhaust it.'

Keeping the motivation levels high, says Sarko, is a constant struggle. 'When you build your world yourself, no one can keep it alive but you, and if you slack, it can come crashing down.' If she gets stuck in 'non-doing' mode, Sarko says she either spends time with other creatives to find inspiration, or makes a bet with herself or a friend. 'I say, "If I don't work today, then..." The deep-rooted athlete mentality in me doesn't let me lose any bets, so I always get up and do what I have to,' she says.

In order to make a living from her art, which sells for US $1,000 to US $6,000 a piece, Sarko has applied a business mindset to her work. 'I don't just create, I also work hard on selling and marketing my art,' she says. 'If you look at all the greats, starting from Picasso, they knew how to sell their works and present themselves.'

Sarko lives in a small studio apartment in Armenia's buzzing capital city Yerevan, which she renovated with friends on a minimal budget. She refurbished her kitchen entirely from recycled materials, and enjoys making her own clothes with natural dyes. 'Everything I do is related to creating,' she says. 'I have no fixed schedule, no boss, no forced obligations. Sometimes I have lots of money, sometimes not so much, but I am constantly doing new projects that keep me excited and happy.'

*Sarko self-portrait*, 2014, oil and watercolour

*Unnoticed*, 2018, metal mesh with canvas backdrop

Sarko's tips to
*make a living living*:

- Don't be too romantic about making art. You still have to <u>be very organized and disciplined</u>, and keep educating yourself if you want to be successful.

- <u>The biggest teachers are books and inspiring speakers.</u> With the internet and YouTube, they're easy to access.

- If you don't make much money, <u>spend less</u> and you'll be fine.

sarkomeene.com
@sarkomeene

## Rohan Hoole and Isabel Kücke

The sustainable designers
on evolving from failure

*'Being adaptable
and learning from
your mistakes is
everything.'*

Creating the biggest business possible was never the goal for Berlin-based creatives Rohan Hoole and Isabel Kücke. Soon after the couple met and fell in love in Mumbai, India – where Rohan had been working as a videographer for *Vogue* and *GQ*, and Isabel was producing hand embroidery for the likes of Prada and Louis Vuitton – they decided they wanted to create a life and business together that had sustainability at its core.

'Working in India, we saw first-hand all the harmful repercussions of the fashion industry, in terms of environmental damage and unfair exploitation of workers,' says Isabel, explaining the inception of their sustainable, radically transparent fashion brand, HundHund.

They spent nine months designing, finding fabric suppliers and factories, building the corporate identity and more, then used their savings to launch their first collection from their apartment. 'It didn't do well, because it was this weird compromise between the two of us without any real aligned identity,' admits Rohan. 'We were pretty close to bankruptcy, having gone through all our savings, but we got on the same page and created a second collection that expressed our shared vision. The day after we put it online, sales were eight times as high.' Eighteen months after that, the couple were finally able to start paying themselves a salary.

The shared vision that eventually led to these profits was largely based around getting their customers thinking about sustainability. 'We also wanted to be part of a community of people who make things and care about the way they make them,' says Rohan.

Moving into a sustainable building called Lobe Block in 2018 allowed them to do just that. The building encompasses their combined studio and store and their apartment, and has connected them to creatives including natural winemakers and sustainable shoemakers, who they have collaborated and thrown events with. 'When we were building our studio, we had very little money, but we collaborated with furniture- and light-makers who were just happy to be making something with other creatives,' says Rohan.

Lobe Block also includes a yoga studio and community garden where Rohan and Isabel keep bees that they tend in their down time, and is close to dog parks where they regularly walk their whippet dog Ella Fitz. Building this life outside work has become increasingly important for the couple. 'Having your own business means that all your decisions are yours to own,' says Rohan. 'That comes with a lot of weight and stress, but it's also an extraordinary freedom and very fulfilling.'

It also means they can travel when they want, often jumping on highly reduced airline error fares. 'Being able to escape, somewhere we can unplug ourselves on a relatively frequent basis, helps immensely with the creative process,' says Rohan.

Rohan and Isabel's tips to *make a living living*:

- <u>Don't overthink projects</u> before you begin them. You learn the most by actually doing the thing.

- Make sure to <u>carve out time for yourself</u>, otherwise you'll burn out.

- <u>Get a dog.</u> They force you to spend time outside and step out of your work brain.

hundhund.com
@hundvonhund

# Hold weekly recap sessions

As surf camp founder Yenifer says, weekly self-meetings are critical for staying on top of goals and progress when you're your own boss. Your goals could be anything from 'make another £100' or 'approach a possible mentor' to 'take a workshop'. Plug these meetings into your calendar notifications and make them non-negotiable.

This is a great way of marking your achievements, discovering how to be more efficient, and working out whether you're putting too much or too little on your plate. Think practically about the way you work every day: working in 90-minute bursts with 20-minute breaks really works for some; the Pomodoro Technique of 25-minute sessions separated by short breaks is better for others. Find the flow that works for you and commit to it.

**YOUR FIRST SESSION**

Week one is an anomaly since future sessions will begin with reviewing last week's goals. Write down the goals you want to achieve during your first week. Below each goal, list the steps that will get you there.

# PLAN

Write down the goals you want to achieve this week, adding to those that you kept from last week. Next, write the steps you need to take to help you achieve the goals, making sure they are do-able. Ask yourself how you will structure each day to achieve your goals.

Make a copy of this list and stick it where you can see it each day, because staying accountable to yourself is key.

# REVIEW

Review last week's goals. Decide which goals to keep and which to discard, either eliminating completely or breaking down any that were overly ambitous or that don't align with your overall purpose.

Review your budget and your work hours: too few, too many?

## Colin Hudon

The tea company founder
on ignoring the cynics

# 'Give yourself permission to disregard what other people think.'

Finding the courage to do what makes us happy can often be the biggest hurdle to building a creatively fulfilling life. Just ask Colin Hudon, who had to learn to silence the sceptics in order to pursue his twin passions of tea and Chinese medicine.

'It took me most of my twenties to arrive at a place where I didn't care what people thought of me, and to pursue a path that felt authentic,' says the 38-year-old American.

With a degree in literature and philosophy under his belt, in his twenties Colin worked for the Consulate General of Canada in the agricultural sphere. He then worked for a sustainability start-up called Greenopia in San Francisco, before launching his own tech company, Goodlife, which folded during the 2007–8 financial crisis. Disenchanted by the stress and pressure involved in these jobs, Colin, who had peripheral interests in t'ai chi, chi kung and tea ceremony, decided to study Chinese medicine.

When he started telling friends and family about this, however, he was often ridiculed. 'The response was usually, "Give me a break, you can't make a living selling snake oil and waving crystal wands"', he says. Owning a tea company, meanwhile, was 'dismissed as something a bored, wealthy housewife does in her spare time'.

Colin chose to disregard these criticisms and in 2009 began studying Chinese medicine and, simultaneously, tea, which led him to start his company Living Tea in 2010.

As an entrepreneur, Colin jokes that he's one of those 'crazy people who work 100 hours a week so they don't have to

work 40 for someone else'. Yet because he's his own boss, in between managing Living Tea and seeing patients through his Chinese medicine practice, he is also able to travel to Asia several times a year, trekking through the mountains to source rare teas and tea-ware for Living Tea.

Colin is most appreciative of the contribution his work enables him to make to his community, via things like acupuncture, dietary guidance, tea ceremony and t'ai chi. 'It's a nice sentiment to want to help others, and there are certainly things we all have to offer, but I am deeply grateful that I have some tangible tools to support people.'

Colin's tips to
*make a living living*:

- Building anything
  from scratch requires
  crazy amounts of work,
  attention, sacrifice and
  focus. It's easy to run out
  of steam unless you <u>avoid
  the 'noise' of naysayers.</u>

- <u>Never make compromises
  for the sake of short-term
  profit.</u> People will sense it
  and mistrust you.

- <u>Seek really good advice</u>
  from people who properly
  understand the central
  tenets of your business.
  Taking advice from the
  unwise is itself unwise.

livingtea.net
@livingtea

# Amber Tamm

The horticulturalist
on overcoming adversity

'A strong vision – one that might even change the world – will push you forward.'

No matter how intense our struggles, there's always a way to rise from the ashes and build a bright future. Proof of this lies in the story of Amber Tamm, who, when she was 18, suffered intense trauma when her mother was murdered by her father. Instead of letting the pain destroy her, however, she used it as motivation.

'After my mum died I became very silent. Then, after two months of not talking or doing much, I went outside into nature and immediately felt that was what I needed. I went straight out and spent all the money I had, US $1,000 at the time, on plants.'

Amber had been working as a teacher of teen programmes at the Whitney Museum of American Art, but decided to quit that job to pursue the thing she knew could make her happy. 'My mother's death made me re-evaluate everything,' says the 24-year-old New Yorker, who grew up in an underprivileged neighbourhood in Brooklyn. 'I was making good money at the Whitney Museum and from the outside it looked perfect, but I was tremendously unhappy,' she says.

Amber took off travelling across America for two and a half years, learning about horticulture on farms, creating green walls for businesses and completing a farming programme in Hawai'i. While learning to farm, Amber says she often received sexist remarks. 'I'd be making a green wall and some guy would ask me if I knew how to use a certain tool, or if I knew what I was doing,' she says. 'It's an attitude that's pretty constant in farming and landscaping.' It was a time, however, that she also describes as deeply therapeutic. 'Each time I planted something, I felt I was bringing my trauma to the soil and it was turning it into food. That was so healing.'

Today, Amber makes a living through horticultural work, landscape architecture, floral design and urban farming in New York, and runs a variety of floral and horticultural workshops. 'I want to inspire people to grow their own food, particularly individuals on lower incomes who don't have much access to fresh food,' she says. 'That's why I offer my workshops on a sliding price scale, so people of colour, low-income individuals and small businesses can access my services. It's also why I share my path on Instagram,

to let black people in my age range understand they can do what they love by creating their own path.'

There are months when cashflow is low, and Amber still needs to supplement her income with part-time work as a baker. Her vision of empowering her community, however, keeps her moving forward with her horticultural work. 'If every person grew one thing and came together to share, then we wouldn't be damaging the earth as much and there would be a greater sense of community.'

Amber's tips to
*make a living living*:

• <u>Talk about your ideas</u> to
a friend or a therapist –
it helps you gain clarity.

• A <u>side job</u> can support you
financially, expand your
skill set and help you meet
new people.

• <u>Spend time in green
spaces</u>, like botanic or
community gardens, and
use indoor plants. They
positively affect mind,
body and spirit.

ambertamm.com
@ambertamm

**Jatinder Singh Durhailay**

The painter and musician
on being patient

'*Develop the patience to learn and improve, one step at a time.*'

Cultivating the necessary skills to make a living doing something you love takes time, patience and diligence, says the London-based painter and musician Jatinder Singh Durhailay.

The 30-year-old, whose artworks exploring Indian Sikh culture are sold and exhibited worldwide, and who has released two albums fusing Indian and Western music, says his success has depended on learning and improving, little by little. 'Indian classical music takes a lot of repetition, and one composition can take months of practising before it's ready, which is very similar to painting,' he says. 'This has taught me to respect the cost of improvement.'

When deciding to pursue art as a career, Jatinder says he 'fell in love with the creative lifestyle of an artist' as much as with the art forms of painting and drawing themselves. Having finished a university degree in digital media design and graphic communication, he realized he didn't want to be confined by the conventions that would probably have surrounded a graphic design career. 'I wanted to work for myself, arrange my daily life, and pursue a career working with my hands,' he says. 'I never paid too much attention to what others thought of my career decisions; I felt too passionate about pursuing a career in the arts and I love to learn. Now my daily life is surrounded by engaging learning, and improving one step at a time.'

By teaching himself how to paint, with the help of tips he learned while working as an assistant to the artist Conor Harrington in London, Jatinder created the artistic lifestyle he had imagined. He sold his first artworks on Tumblr and Instagram, which led to an increasing number of commissions from clients, and to being exhibited in the UK and abroad. In 2012 he also started recording his music, sharing it on the online platform Soundcloud and performing small ticketed concerts and workshops.

Today Jatinder makes a stable income from selling his paintings, prints and CDs direct from his studio and from his online shop, and he and his wife, the French artist Johanna Tagada, split their year between London, rural Tamil Nadu in South India and the various destinations they travel to. 'The art business definitely requires certain sacrifices, particularly financial security,' he says, noting that things like not drinking alcohol, eating a vegan diet and not having a car all help save extra money. 'But we are happy with little, we have a lot of fun every day and really, the excess of material belongings can only bring stress.' .

Jatinder's tips to
*make a living living*:

- You won't know until
  you try.

- Try to <u>find more positivity
  within yourself</u>.

- Remember that you can
  <u>bring creativity to whatever
  you do</u>.

jatindersinghdurhailay.com
@jatindersinghdurhailay

*I'll be Your Sportsgirl*, 2018, gouache on hemp paper

*I'll be Your Sportsman*, 2018, gouache on hemp paper

# Get a creative practice

Setting aside time to let our brains wander is essential for keeping the creative juices flowing, so we need to make time for creative play every day. Try these three exercises, then try coming up with creative practice ideas that resonate with your interests and talents.

## MORNING PAGES JOURNALLING

Since reading Julia Cameron's *The Artist's Way* a decade ago, I've dedicated 20 minutes most days to 'morning pages'. This is free-writing, simply keeping your hand moving without thinking too hard about what you're writing until time is up or three pages are full. Most of the time it won't be Shakespeare, but this isn't about making great work. It's about being creative even when you don't feel like it.

# RIGHT BRAIN DRAWING

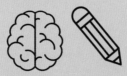

Draw something with your non-dominant hand – for most of us, our left hand. This hand links to the right side of your brain, where most artistic thinking happens, so you'll be surprised how much more easily imaginative, creative thought flows afterwards.

# PHOTOGRAPHY WALK

Grab your camera and take a 30-minute photography walk. Pick a simple theme – the colour yellow, say, or circular shapes – and take photos of that theme as you go. The aim is to make you see your familiar surroundings in a new light, and to help you think in an untemplated way more often.

## Morgane Seuillot

The natural winemaker
on finding balance

'Give yourself
some time every
day to recharge
your mind and
body.'

Discovering that Morgane Seuillot owns her own vineyard, Domaine Dandelion in France's Burgundy wine region, you might assume her days involve frolicking among the vines, glass of wine in hand. But they really don't. Instead they involve endless hours of work in both the field and the winery, and a level of focus that can quickly become all-consuming.

'When you run your own company, it becomes so important for you that you can forget about the essentials of life,' says the 28-year-old. 'You tend not to take enough time to look after your body, take care of your family or visit friends, but really they are the key to your success.'

Raised in Burgundy, Morgane studied winemaking at university in France and the UK, then spent a year doing traineeships in Australian vineyards, before using her life savings to buy two hectares of vines in Burgundy in 2016. 'I didn't have a penny left, and for the first year I continued working a few hours a week for winemaker friends to make ends meet,' she says.

Morgane does most of the work for Domaine Dandelion herself, from harvesting and pruning to making the wine in the most natural way possible, in a winery she shares with two friends. 'We all help each other and share,' she says. 'We watch each other's barrels and tanks when we go on holidays and split bills, so it's also a good way of saving money.'

While the lifestyle of a winemaker can often be romanticized, Morgane says it's far from easy. Her vines suffered bad frost damage in 2016, for example, which meant she didn't make any money from her wine that first year. Because the work is seasonal, she can also work long days for months at a time without any time off. And yet, Morgane describes herself as 'blessed'.

'Winemaking is ten jobs in one so I never get bored,' she says. 'I also love following the seasons. Working with nature and being in tune with it feels almost like a luxury these days.' After harvest in September Morgane is able to indulge her love of travel, and in winter when work in the vineyard slows down there's time for cooking with friends, looking after her garden, chickens and horses, and working on the rundown 1800s presbytery she and her boyfriend bought and are renovating themselves.

**Morgane's tips to** *make a living living*:

- Make the most of your down time and <u>take care of your body</u>.

- Find a way to <u>combine both intellectual and manual work</u>, even if it's just looking after a vegetable patch. You will be mentally healthier.

- <u>Foster community.</u> Living your dream can be hard work: it's important to have people to help you along the way.

@domaine.dandelion

# Renu Kashyap

The stylist and author
on collaborating with the right people

# 'Team work really does make the dream work.'

Renu Kashyap is a woman who keeps many balls in the air. The 42-year-old Amsterdam native runs a bed and breakfast with her DJ husband in the Ibiza countryside, is a freelance fashion editor for the likes of *Vogue* Netherlands, co-authored the coffee-table book *Ibiza Bohemia* and runs quarterly mother–daughter retreats.

Keeping all of these ventures afloat may sound exhausting. But because they're all within the styling sphere, and since Renu has found trustworthy, reliable partners to collaborate with, she has been able to build a relaxed way of life around them. 'I used to be very fast-paced,' she says of her former life as a magazine fashion director in Amsterdam. 'I was a workaholic and never in the moment.' Craving a slower lifestyle and warmer climate, in 2012 Renu quit her job and moved with her husband and their then two-year-old daughter to Ibiza.

'When we moved to Ibiza, we didn't have much because we started from scratch,' she says. 'But we didn't need much because the quality of life is super high, the weather's always nice and there's beautiful nature, so you don't need to constantly entertain yourself with things that cost money.'

When carving out income streams in Ibiza, Renu worked with both the location and her styling skills and contacts. She and her husband invested their savings into renting a seven-bedroom home in the countryside, which Renu transformed into their bed and breakfast Casa Amore, where they also live. The changes she made to the property were mainly superficial, including new furniture, linens and lighting, so overheads were low, and she has devised a cost-effective way of maintaining the house. 'Once a year we put an ad on Facebook for people to exchange working on the house for a holiday in it, so we save on construction costs,' she says.

Renu describes Casa Amore as her 'creative hub', since she also uses it as a location and crew villa for her shoots and as the setting for her retreat, My Daughter and Me, which she runs with a friend. 'Finding good partners who complement your skill set is so important,' she says.

Renu's tips to
*make a living living*:

- If you want to get into the property game, try to <u>find partners to help you</u> finance this idea.

- <u>Write a business plan, and work with a graphic designer</u> to make the layout as appealing and clear as possible, to help get investors as enthusiastic as you are.

- If you want to change your life, <u>start by trying different things</u> and meeting as many new people as possible.

angeliquehoorn.com
@renukashyap_stylist
@casaamoreibiza

## Angus McDiarmid

The potter
on continually learning

'Ask questions
all the time.
There's so much
knowledge in our
communities.'

Step inside the handmade bush home of the Australian potter
Angus McDiarmid and you would assume he has half a dozen skilled trades
under his belt.

Except that aside from pottery, he doesn't. The effervescent 31-year-old taught himself everything he needed to know to turn a shack into a pottery studio, gallery and home for himself, his wife Bridget and their one-year-old son. Through meeting timber workers in his community and asking them loads of questions, Angus learned to make the furniture, cupboards, decking and doors out of local wood, to craft the lights, tiles and kitchen sink from terracotta, and to do all the plumbing and electrical wiring himself. 'People tell themselves they can only be one thing, but the joy of life lies in learning new things,' he says.

Angus's search for a more creative life began in 2011 when, after quitting his commerce and arts degree, he embarked on a nine-month cycling trip through South America, then travelled to India. 'I remember drinking chai from a clay cup in Himachal Pradesh one day and asking, "Where are these made?" I was told there was a pottery village nearby so I went straight there, and ended up doing a six-month pottery course there.' When he returned to Australia, Angus Googled wood-fired potters, found a nearby studio and simply turned up. 'I was like, "Hi, I want to be a potter!" The owner handed me a book about the chemical components of glazing and told me to come back in a week. I studied every page, and ended up staying with that studio for two years.'

Angus is now Australia's youngest wood-fired potter. He works

completely without electricity in his outdoor home studio, which sits next to his small gallery space. This means he can make more sales directly from home and online, which translates to more income per piece since he's not paying the standard 30 to 50 per cent commission taken by stores. He makes his pieces from blended local clay that he digs himself and shapes on kick wheels, and fires his hand-built kiln with local wood he splits by hand.

Although he loves the raw, handmade aspects of wood-firing, he admits it comes with risks. Numerous times, Angus has

unpacked his kiln after spending eight to ten weeks making, only to discover that AU $15,000 (US $10,600) worth of product has completely shattered, owing partially to the volatility of the local clay he uses. The work can also become mentally and physically taxing, with Angus often creating 100 pieces a day to ensure the mortgage gets paid.

Mostly, however, Angus finds great joy and peace in his work. 'I spend more time with kangaroos and chickens than I do with humans. I make pots all day long while listening to music, and time just disappears.'

Angus's tips to
*make a living living*:

- Remember: <u>your ego is always three steps ahead of your practical skills.</u>

- <u>Teach yourself</u> how to create the things in life you want.

- Learn to unlearn. <u>Constantly ask yourself, 'How can I do that better?'</u>

panpottery.com
@panpottery

# Jeanne de Kroon

The ethical fashion designer
on working for a cause

'Find something
you believe in
that the world
needs – build
your business
from that.'

Sometimes it's a single moment that brings our life's purpose into focus. For Jeanne de Kroon, founder of the ethical fashion brand Zazi Vintage, that moment came during a trip to Nepal in 2014.

'I was feeling really lost, studying philosophy at university in Berlin but mostly partying, when I booked a ticket to Nepal,' says the Dutch 26-year-old. 'I was walking down an alley dressed in black when a local lady grabbed my hand and said, "Your eyes look like celebration, but your outfit says no." She took me to a vintage shop, put me in this glittery Bollywood outfit, and I immediately felt myself again.'

Wanting to recreate that self-affirming moment for other women, and having become disillusioned by the unethical production practices and waste often generated by the fashion industry, Jeanne decided to create her company, Zazi Vintage. Despite her lack of money and resources, she was passionate about building a business with a core purpose.

'Knowing that fashion is our planet's second most polluting industry, I didn't want to create any new garments,' she says. Instead, while travelling to India using money she saved from teaching yoga, Jeanne spent EUR 250 (US $280) on exotic vintage dresses, most of which were supply-chain waste or dead stock. Back in her student bedroom in Berlin, she photographed herself in the pieces and used Facebook, Etsy and markets to sell them. She then reinvested the profits into more vintage, started an Instagram account and spent EUR 30 (US $34) building a Squarespace website, the same website she still uses. As profits increased, Jeanne began designing her own pieces, which she trained and employed disadvantaged women in India to make for her. Her first collection included just seven dresses, which she paid

a friend EUR 50 (US $56) to shoot for her. Jeanne then used every fashion contact she had to help push the Zazi message into the media. Within a year the brand was featured in *Vogue* Germany and was picked up by MatchesFashion, and Jeanne was speaking on sustainable fashion panels alongside the likes of Stella McCartney.

Today Jeanne lives a largely nomadic life, and employs more than 50 disadvantaged women in villages across Central Asia, Afghanistan and India to produce her Zazi creations. 'I think a big reason for unhappiness is when you don't feel you're giving your time, the most precious thing in life, to something you believe in,' she says. 'The only thing I want is to be able to support the work of more amazing women around the world.'

Jeanne's tips to
*make a living living*:

- <u>Start your day with a
  five-minute meditation,</u>
  to help you stay centred.

- Never make compromises,
  and <u>always stay true to
  your initial intention</u>.

- <u>Journalling is a great way
  of staying focused</u> on
  what you want to achieve
  each day.

zazi-vintage.com
@zazi.vintage

# *Make a mood board*

Building a creative career, one outside societal norms, takes intention, tenacity and, most importantly, a crystal-clear vision. Mood boarding can be a really helpful tool for identifying this vision, including the kind of energy, community and work you want to attract.

Buy a poster-sized piece of cardboard, grab a stack of old magazines, some scissors and a tube of glue and start cutting and pasting images that speak to the kind of life you want to move towards. These can be pictures of places and people, but also colours, landscapes, interiors and even found objects like dried flowers, coins or photographs. Next, add words that capture the qualities you're looking for in your life – see opposite.

This process will not only help you stay true to your vision, but will also get the creative juices flowing and pull you out of creative ruts when they arise. Whenever you find yourself wondering if a decision is the right one, you can return to your mood board and get some clarity as to whether it is aligned or not.

Paste on your mood board any images or found objects that evoke the kind of energy you want to be surrounded by, then add words that inspire you. Here are some of mine.

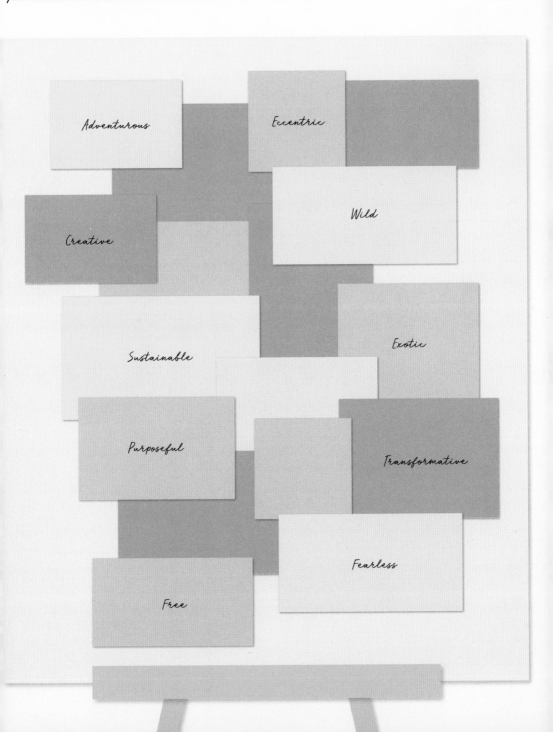

Adventurous

Eccentric

Wild

Creative

Sustainable

Exotic

Purposeful

Transformative

Fearless

Free

## Amanda Callan and Andrew Morris

The soap and sauce makers
on putting lifestyle first

*'Allow yourself to fall in love with a space and let your vision grow around it.'*

When Amanda Callan and Andrew Morris first saw the old country church they now call home on Australia's mid-east coast, they knew it had to be theirs.

Never mind that it didn't have a kitchen or bedrooms, was set on a floodplain in a country town where they knew no one, or that neither of them had full-time work. Oh, and that Amanda was pregnant with their first child. 'It was just so beautiful, we decided then and there that we'd do everything we could to build a life here,' says Amanda.

Being on a floodplain, the property was cheap, and the couple said yes to any work that would pay the bills. 'We weren't picky,' says Amanda, who did bookkeeping for local farmers' markets while Andrew, a guitarist, did odd gigs, made food products and gardened to make ends meet.

For extra cash, Amanda, who was studying naturopathy at the time, started making natural soap and selling it in a roadside stall in front of their church. Local shops soon started stocking the soaps and little by little, as the couple slowly renovated their church by hand, their business evolved, with Andrew soon making condiments and pickles to add to their offering.

'We started making our products simply because we loved doing it, and the business grew from there,' says Andrew of their business, Church Farm General Store. 'We now spend our days doing things we actually like doing. It makes us feel good, we're not harming the environment, and we have a good amount of free time.'

The couple have created a passive income source through a rental apartment they built in their garden, and have purposefully kept Church Farm General Store small, selling mainly at farmers' markets and local stores, as well as running soap-making workshops. This way, they have plenty of time to spend with their two young kids, to surf every day, garden in their vegetable patches and take trips in their vintage caravan.

'We could make the business bigger if we worked harder, but we like the way it is now, so we're not working on it all day, every day,' says Amanda. 'We love our business, but we also love our kids and just hanging out.'

Amanda and Andrew's tips to *make a living living*:

- **Figure out what lifestyle you want**, then find work to fit in with that, rather than the other way around.

- **Write all your wild ideas down**, so you can get really clear on what you want.

- **Trust your instincts.**

churchfarmgeneralstore.com
@churchfarmgeneralstore

## Manon Meyering

The writer and energy worker
on appreciating the journey

# 'A creative life is a never-ending journey, so learn to trust the path.'

Manon Meyering believes that in order to build a creatively fulfilling life,
you have to learn to enjoy the journey and its sometimes surprising turns,
rather than becoming overly focused on the end goal.

Her career path took its first unexpected turn in her twenties when, despite having studied international business and languages at university, she followed her instincts and started working in magazines, the industry that had most excited her since she was a child. 'Despite not having the "right" qualifications, I was eager to learn and determined to stay,' she says.

She started as a coordinator, then moved into positions including stylist, editor and image director, before finally landing a job as a fashion, beauty and lifestyle director for a European glossy magazine at the age of 27. After she faced health issues, Manon's path shifted again as she began freelancing, to give herself a more flexible schedule and more time to follow her spiritual path.

Manon started training with a spiritual teacher, and in less than a year started running life-coaching and energy-healing sessions, and wellbeing retreats for companies and private groups on evenings and weekends. In that same period she took on a role as a director at another magazine, one that saw her travelling from Argentina and Thailand to India and beyond, and meeting and interviewing celebrities including Alicia Keys and Beyoncé.

In 2014, Manon's path changed course once more when she and her husband moved to Kenya to become parents to their adopted Kenyan son Micah. In the beginning they lived from their savings,

giving themselves time to connect with both their son and the local community, which led Manon to create her online not-for-profit handcraft store Naramatisho.

Today, Manon and her family live between the Dutch countryside and a beach house they bought on Kenya's south coast, which they rent out when they're back in the

Netherlands and vice versa, for extra income. Manon continues to combine her healing sessions with her writing and editing work for Dutch women's magazines, for which she still travels regularly. 'The contrast couldn't be starker, but the mix of creativity and spirituality serves my "yin yang balance" well,' she says.

Manon's tips to
*make a living living:*

- <u>Don't compare yourself to others.</u> Your uniqueness is your power.

- <u>Look for things that bring you greater delight</u>, instead of specific jobs or talents, and make a career out of those.

- If you want a freelance writing life, pitch ideas to magazines and websites. <u>Practice your writing on blogs or social media.</u>

# 'It's a great time to be an artist because you can get really creative about bringing in extra money.'

Large-scale creative projects can take years to finish, swallowing large chunks of time, money and energy. This is something the filmmaker Jess Bianchi discovered after completing his first feature film *Given*, which was released to critical acclaim in 2016.

Following a professional surfer couple and their two small children on a journey across 15 countries, the film took Jess and his team 14 months of travel and three years of sporadic editing to create. 'After *Given*, I felt as though I'd been spat out of the belly of the beast. I put so much of myself into it that my whole life, especially my health, almost fell apart afterwards,' says the 38-year-old American-Italian. 'Since then I've decided that ideally, I'd like to make a movie every five years.'

In order to make this a reality, Jess has created some clever additional income sources to support himself as he slowly chips away at his films. Before starting *Given* he invested his savings in a small piece of land in Hawai'i, where he grew up. The simple cottage he had built on it is where he, his wife and their two-year-old son now live part-time. They rent it out when they're in LA.

While making *Given*, Jess founded a boutique production company called Avocados and Coconuts, which helped bring in revenue to keep funding *Given* and which he has since sold. He also continues to receive income from *Given*, through selling it to Netflix and on sites including iTunes.

After finishing film school in his mid-twenties, Jess jumped straight into advertising, getting an entry-level position at the film company AutoFuss. 'It was a young company at the time and I learned so much there, because they moved me around to different positions including PA, grip [technician providing camera support], photographer, editor and cinematographer,' he says.

Jess worked in the advertising world for four more years, but although the work was well paid and Jess was putting his skills to use, it started to feel creatively unfulfilling. 'I felt so lame and un-artistic making commercials for companies I didn't really care about that I thought, "The next thing I do, I'm going to put my heart and soul into it."' He took some time off to regroup, which is when he reconnected with a childhood friend who ended up being the central character in *Given*, teaching him the importance of following his instincts.

The internet, says Jess, is critical to the success of much creative work in the modern world. '*Given* would have never made it on to Netflix had somebody not seen it online and fallen in love with it,' he says. 'You can rent out houses online, sell whatever you want on sites, the possibilities are limitless.'

Jess's tips to
*make a living living*:

- A <u>second income</u> outside your creative passion can help ease financial pressure.

- When you're doing creative work, <u>staying physically fit</u> is really important.

- <u>Collaborate with other creatives</u>, especially in different fields, so you're not just drawing from your own energy.

giventhemovie.com
@jess__bianchi

# Choose your journey

Where we live and work can dictate who we're surrounded by, the pace of our lives, the state of our mental and physical health and more. One of the best creativity boosts you might be able to give yourself, then, is to travel.

Plan a trip. Replant yourself somewhere that surrounds you with more dynamic levels of creativity, a more like-minded community, and a physical environment, climate and culture you feel you really belong in. This can be as simple as a two-day road trip, or as complex as planning a move to the other side of the world.

Ask yourself: what do I need from this journey? Is it nature immersion, an injection of spirituality, the inspiration of art, culture or colour, or simply for your mind to unfurl on a long road trip? This table, while by no means exhaustive, will help you choose your destination/s and create a trip that will draw the most creative juice from you.

If you are on a tight budget, discovering a new place closer to home can be just as creatively rewarding as setting foot on a far-flung destination. Also, whether you're journeying near or far, consider your environmental impact. Locally, try to use low-carbon public transport where possible. If flying is necessary, look into carbon-offsetting schemes, like those at mossy.earth.

## ROAD TRIP

Long stretches of highway, inspiring small towns and all that reflection time, road trips are the ultimate reboot.

### ISRAEL
**Jerusalem to the Dead Sea** – via Masada and Ein Gedi oasis (three days)
**Negev Desert Tour** – stopping at Ramon Crater and small farms (three days)
**Haifa to Safed** – art-filled mystical mountaintop town (single day)

### IRELAND
**Wild Atlantic Way** – Cork to Donegal, jagged cliffs, epic bays (two weeks)
**Skellig Ring** – seabirds, colourful houses, walking trails (single day)
**Causeway Coastal Route** – Belfast to the walled city of Londonderry (two days)

### AMERICA
**Charleston to New Orleans** – Deep South (three days)
**California's Pacific Coast Highway** – San Francisco to San Diego (three days)
**Route 66** – cross-country, including Chicago and Grand Canyon (two weeks)

### AUSTRALIA
**The Nullarbor** – goldfields of Western Australia to the Eyre Peninsula (five days)
**Gibb River Road** – rugged Kimberley wilderness, WA (six days)
**Tasmania's East Coast** – Orford to St Helens (weekend)

### NZ
**Auckland to Coromandel** – stunning beaches and coves (three days return)
**Christchurch to Queenstown** – via Lake Tekapo, Mt Cook, Lake Wanaka (four days)
**Auckland to Wellington** – Maori culture, vineyards, hot springs (four days)

## ART / CULTURE

Immerse yourself in art and culture and you'll likely expand your global creative network, too.

### BERLIN
**Kreuzberg** – heart of the bohemian counter-culture scene
**Museum Island** – five world-class museums
**East Side Gallery** – section of the Berlin Wall, world's largest open-air gallery

### BARCELONA
**Gaudi architecture** – La Sagrada Familia, Park Güell, Casa Batlló
**Concert at Palace of Catalan Music**
**Gothic Quarter** – then Montjuic hilltop for city views

### PARIS
**Centre Pompidou** – grande dame of Paris's contemporary art scene
**Cinémathèque Française** – film history and avant-garde screenings
**Concert at Philharmonie de Paris** – home to the Paris orchestra

### AMSTERDAM
**Rijksmuseum** – Dutch art, middle ages to today
**Jordaan** – explore offbeat galleries and vintage shops in this bohemian quarter
**De Ceuvel** – former industrial site, houseboats turned design ateliers, cafes

### LONDON
**Shakespeare's Globe** – open-air theatre
**Tate Modern** – four art museums in one
**Barbican Centre** – performing arts venue

## SPIRIT

Whether you choose a pilgrimage, retreat or spiritual festival, these journeys will help soothe the soul.

### INDIA
Bodh Gaya – study with the Buddhists
Varanasi – meditate with the sadhus
Rishikesh – yoga in the Himalayas

### INDONESIA
Bali – attend Ubud Spirit Festival
Java – Borobudur, world's biggest Buddhist monument
Nusa Penida – visit underground caverns that house seven shrines

### SRI LANKA
Talalla – beach yoga retreat
Dambulla – Buddhist cave temples, then climb Sigiriya rock fortress
Nuwara Eliya – R&R in Sri Lanka's tea country

### BHUTAN
Paro – hike to Tiger's Nest Monastery
Uma Paro retreat – yoga, massage and Ayurveda
Increase your Gross National Happiness – Bhutan focuses on this, not GDP

### JAPAN
Hokkaido – ice floes and soul-soothing onsen bathing
Tokyo – start the Nakasendo Way 10-night walking pilgrimage to Kyoto
Kyoto – for temples and teahouses, gardens and geishas

## NATURE

Nature immersion gets the creative juices flowing and gives you that crucial sense of wonder for the planet.

### AFRICA
Serengeti – for the Great Migration
Ethiopia – Simien Mountains to find the elusive Ethiopian wolf
Botswana – world's largest elephant population

### CANADA
Churchill – meet polar bears
Newfoundland – hike the remote Long Range Traverse
Banff – see glacier-fed Lake Louise

### ICELAND
Northern Lights – mid-September to early April
Blue Lagoon – soak in hot mineral springs
Reynisfjara – famous black sand beach

### CHILE
Atacama Desert – salt flats, hot springs, geysers, flamingos
Torres del Paine National Park – Patagonian hiking
Elqui Valley – one of the world's best astro-tourism destinations

### GUATEMALA
Acatenango – overnight volcano hike
Semuc Champey – natural pools hidden in the jungle
Lake Atitlan – ringed by volcanoes and Mayan villages

## COLOUR

Colour boosts mood and productivity – and just makes life more fun. Chase it, in the most flamboyant countries on earth.

### MEXICO
San Cristóbal de las Casas – turmeric-hued highland town
Oaxaca City – heart of Mexican folk art
Tulum – Mayan ruins on turquoise beaches

### CUBA
Old Havana – explore on foot
Trinidad – Spanish colonial settlement between mountains and ocean
Havana Jazz Festival – January each year

### MOROCCO
Chefchaouen – explore the blue city
Atlas Mountains – hike through rust-coloured mountains
Marrakesh – shop the vibrant souks

### TURKEY
Istanbul – Hagia Sophia and the Blue Mosque; hip Beyoglu
Cappadocia – sunrise hot-air balloon ride; stay in a cave
Pamukkale – World Heritage-listed limestone terraces

### PERU
Trek the Ausangate Trail – five days, including the rainbow-coloured mountain
Cusco – quaint cobbled streets and locals in traditional, colourful dress
Choquequirao – the new (and less crowded) Machu Picchu

## ABOUT THE AUTHOR

Nina Karnikowski created a living living by fusing her two passions: writing and travelling. Based in the Australian surf town of Byron Bay, she writes travel stories for newspapers, magazines and websites, focusing on wild, transformative adventures off the beaten track. Nina's travel career has seen her journeying through Mongolia in ex-Russian military vehicles, exploring the Namibian desert in open-sided safari trucks, dodging Antarctic icebergs in an icebreaker ship, speeding through northern India by rail, and beyond, to more than 60 countries. See more of her work at travelswithnina.com, or @travelswithnina on Instagram.

## AUTHOR'S ACKNOWLEDGEMENTS

My deepest thanks to everyone featured in this book, for their time and patience, for inviting me into their worlds, and for doing the work they do. I only hope I have done their inspiring stories justice.

Thank you to my husband, Peter Windrim, for his endless support, keen eye, beautiful photographic work, and for always being my first reader. To my mum, Mary, for always caring about this project, even when she didn't entirely understand what it was about.

A special thank you to my editor, Andrew Roff, for his attention to detail, boundless enthusiasm, and for always helping me bring things back down to earth. You are the best editor I could have hoped for. To the rest of the team at Laurence King Publishing, especially Mariana Sameiro, who did an incredible job designing this book. And to Henry Carroll, without you this book wouldn't exist – thank you for envisaging it before I could.

## PICTURE CREDITS